Two Spoiled Rotten Collies Live Here

(And They Are Not The First)

Pets & Other Critters
I Have Known

Beverly J. Hess

Illustrations by Richard L. Caplinger

ISBN 1-880710-50-1

Monterey Pacific Publishing
San Francisco

ii

To Frank

**Who Gives Me The Strength
To Be Who I Am**

This book is dedicated to the wonderful collies that I have had and currently have, beginning with the beautiful - Princess 1966 - 1979

the comforting - Randi   1975 - 1988
the intelligent - Sabra   1982 - 1993
and the spoiled babies:
Tangie 1993
&
Lexie 1993

And to the unforgettable Beauregard 1974-1989

And to the memory of Lady who started it all.

Contents

Contents

Contents

Contents

Contents

Introduction

My love affair with Collies began both with the TV series "Lassie" and earlier while spending summers on my grandmother's farm in the company of a beautiful male collie named "Lad."

I always dreamed of having a whole house full of collies and thought that I would one day breed them. It took until my adult years to understand that I could never breed collies and make any money because I would never be able to let any of them go.

I've satisfied myself over the years with always having at least one beautiful, loyal, intelligent collie to brighten my days.

After I married and moved to Florida, my collie love affair started in earnest when I first met Lady and Prince.

Lady And Prince

I was living in a little town on the panhandle of Florida called Panama City, where my Air Force husband served his enlistment at Tyndall Air Force Base. We were living in a little cottage near the base that was owned by two retired school teachers. Since we didn't have a car, I was left home to "housewife" and do whatever I pleased for the first six months of our stay there. Across the highway on the opposite bay lived a couple who had two collies, Lady and her son, Prince.

Frequently in the afternoon, I would go across the highway and visit with Lady who loved to accompany me down to the water for long walks. She was a gentle, lovely, four-year-old champion beauty who soon became pregnant after a planned mating with another champion male collie in the area.

It was funny, when I was busy and neglected to walk over and visit with Lady, she would very carefully (and against her owner's wishes) cross the highway and come to my door and give one discreet bark to get my attention. When I opened the door, she would take my wrist in her mouth and lead me back across the highway and down to the water for our afternoon walk.

Soon Lady had her puppies, a litter of five lovely, fluffy darlings.

We Face A Tragedy

One afternoon I walked across to see Lady and visit with the two-week-old pups. Lady was not with the puppies and nowhere to be found. I went to the owner's house and when they learned she was not outside with the pups they too became alarmed and we walked down to the water together. There we found Lady lying next to the water very ill. We rushed her to the vet's office, but we were too late. He said that someone had poisoned her because what he found in her system was not something she would have picked up outdoors, but a household poison.

We returned home overwhelmed with the grief and anger of losing Lady in such a horrible, senseless way. Who would have poisoned such a sweet, gentle dog, the obvious new mother of puppies? We found Prince watching over the puppies who by this time were yelping and crying for Mom to come feed them. Now we were really in a mess. How were we going to raise these poor orphaned puppies? Dot and I worked out a schedule. I set my clock for every two hours and scurried across the highway to help feed the little darlings using doll baby bottles. Somehow, over the next three weeks we managed to keep all of the puppies alive and weaned them off the bottle and onto puppy chow. When the dust settled and all was said and done, my neighbors gave me my pick of the litter for helping to save them. I chose a little female, (the smallest of the litter) and the sweetest of them all. We named her Princess in honor of Prince who valiantly helped us guard and protect the puppies after his mother was so senselessly murdered. Her death remained a mystery as no one was ever caught.

We moved soon after acquiring Princess, into a trailer on a private, fenced-in lot. She loved the outside and wanted to play with everything and everyone, making her very popular with the neighborhood children.

When she was about six months old, my husband went out the back gate right about dusk to dump some leaves in the woods. It was obvious that Princess had not seen him go, because when he returned in the almost dark, he heard a rustling noise and a low growl and just had enough light to see her in mid air, mouth open, about to crash into his chest. He only had time to say "Princess!!" She recognized his voice and closed her mouth. We realized that although gentle and sweet natured, she would be fierce in the protection of her humans.

We moved a second time into a little cottage on an inland bay where she found more things to play with. Boats, although fun to ride on, were not allowed into our bay. If they defied her "ferocious" barking and pulled into our dock they had better be prepared as their "payment" to take her for a ride. She would jump in the boat and wait patiently. She was very persistent and usually outlasted the boat owner. They would take her for a short spin around the bay and then she would be happy. It was almost like a "docking fee."

She was not as fond of the water though, and would only swim if thrown overboard. I always had to go in with her because she tired easily in the water and would rest her front paws on my knees between swims. Now they have doggie life preservers which would have been an excellent idea for her, but at the time that was unheard of.

Besides boats she also had a problem with squirrels. She loved to chase them up into the trees and they loved to sit in the branches and chatter at her and throw pine cones down in her direction. I often wondered what would happen if one of them allowed itself to be caught. She was such a gentle soul I doubt

3

if she would know what to do. Her encounters (in a later chapter) with skunks would prove to me she meant no living creature harm.

Across the field on the next street was a day care center for pre-schoolers. I would hear them calling "here Lassie" and had to go outside periodically and call her home. She would be standing at the fence, tail wagging, letting them put their little fingers through the fence to pet her, poke her, pull her ears, whatever they wanted.

One afternoon I heard loud insistent barking and the screeching of birds. Wondering what she had gotten into now, I went outside to find a snake attempting to invade a blue jay nest and eat the eggs. The jays were dive bombing the snake and Princess was barking and charging the snake trying to make it go away. It took every ounce of courage that I could muster but I scared the snake away and made Princess come inside. The fear and repulsion that I had for snakes made that more excitement than I needed for one day.

After a few months in Florida, we purchased a car so that I could find a job and we could do grocery shopping, etc. We still couldn't afford car insurance and therefore were not permitted to drive on the Air Force base. I used to pick my husband up at the front gate when he did the grocery shopping at the base grocery so he wouldn't have to carry the bags while he was trying to hitchhike home. On one particular afternoon

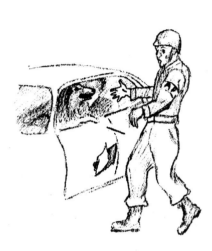

I was parked outside the gate with Princess waiting to pick up hubby and the groceries. An AP (air police) stopped and inquired rather roughly about what I was doing there. I was attempting to explain when over the back seat came my sweet little collie, teeth bared, growling ferociously and snapping at the AP. Again, she felt her family threatened. He backed away from the car about six feet and terminated our conversation, advising me to keep my doors locked while waiting for my husband. What I was thinking and did not say, was that he should be more careful about how he approached cars until he was certain who and what was inside. Imagine if it had been a trained attack dog?

She had another, similar experience years later when I was living in Eastlake, Ohio. A policeman had stopped my car because it matched the description of a getaway car from a bank robbery. He approached the car with a handgun drawn and Princess went crazy - barking and growling and flying against the window. I was too busy trying to hold and quiet her to be frightened, but soon realized I might be in trouble when

5

I saw a second officer approaching with a handgun drawn. After a few minutes the second officer explained the mixup, semi-apologized for stopping me and sent me on the way. Princess, however, wasn't buying into his apology. She didn't stop growling until we were nearly a mile away. And every time after that when she saw a police car she would growl.

When Princess was about eight months old, we noticed that she appeared to be putting on some weight. A trip to the vet confirmed that she was pregnant! How could my baby be having babies? I didn't think she was even old enough to have begun that cycle. Somehow, while I wasn't watching, a nasty, roving Romeo had seduced her.

When she was 10 months old, her puppies were born. She wanted me beside her during the births, but didn't require my assistance. I helped anyway by taking each pup and drying it with a warm towel and placing it near her. She had five pups, four females and one male (the exact same size and sex division as the litter she was from). One look at the little darlings and I knew who the father was. An ugly, yellow, long legged, dirty mutt. How could she have disgraced the family in this way? Where had I gone wrong?

Princess was a good mother and when the pups were ready to be adopted there was no problem finding homes for them. The four little girls were short haired but very cute. The only male had long hair and looked like he might grow up looking somewhat like a collie. We called him "Woolly Bully." My boss at the hospital decided to take him and renamed him "King."

"King Comes Home"

When Princess's puppies were about 10 months old, my boss took a job in Virginia. He called me to ask if I would find "King" another home as they couldn't take him and had been unable to find him a home so far. They were leaving the next day and said they would leave him in their fenced-in yard for me to pick up.

We went over first thing in the morning to get him. I went into the fenced-in yard and didn't see any dog. I called him and called him and looked everywhere, but no dog. I had just about made up my mind that they had changed their minds and taken him, when I heard a little whimper from under the bushes.

I got down to peer under the bush and saw something cowering there. I called to him and he crawled out. He stood up and deja-vu all over again! There (except for the color) stood that nasty, filthy, roaming Romeo that had caused this mess. I said, "King?" He happily wagged a yes. We took him home with  us and were never able to place him with another family until we left Florida when he was almost two. Our friends who had six months more to go on their enlistment wanted to rent our house so we made a package deal. We would put in a good word with our landlord for them and let them have our furniture, but they must also take King. They happily agreed, because King was such a sweetie and mostly because they wanted my house.

"Better Get King, He's Drowning"

The year that we had King was quite an experience. He was sweet and agreeable but totally non-trainable. He never learned what "no" meant. He never learned what "come" meant, he never learned "sit" or "stay" or "down" or anything. He would just look at you, smile and wag his tail. We had to keep him tied outside all the time because he would run away or rather he would wander off. He barely recognized his own name and wouldn't come if you called him. He would just wag his tail and smile.

Drinking was another function King never mastered. He would drink and drink and drink and drink and drink from the water dish, pick his head up and the water would all run out. I guess he must have swallowed enough to keep him alive but it sure didn't look like it.

King loved to swim and would dive off the boat himself. He would swim and swim and then have to be rescued because he had gone too far and was too tired to swim back. If I was water skiing off our beach and he spotted me, he would dive in and try to swim to me. We would have to stop skiing and go rescue King. He would let us pull him into the boat and then wag his tail and smile.

9

Princess Runs Away

One summer when Princess was about two and just after we had gotten King back, my parents came to Florida for vacation. My husband had some leave time coming, so we decided to take a trip with them down into peninsula Florida. We had two of our Air Force buddies stay at the house and watch Princess and King.

We were gone about 10 days and when we returned the dogs seemed very glad to see us. After unloading the car, putting things away and getting settled, we realized Princess was nowhere to be found. This was really scary behavior from "the perfect dog" who never did anything wrong. We took two cars and started driving around looking for her. By this time it was 1:00 in the morning and still no Princess. My husband wanted to quit and start looking again in the morning, but my mother and I went once more to search in the car. As we were driving along the main highway about half a mile from our house, my mother suddenly yelled "there she is!!"

We pulled into a drive-in ice cream stand and there she was, sitting up for some young teenagers who were feeding her corn dogs. I got out of the car and said "Princess!!!" The kids said "oh please don't scold her, she's so smart and pretty." I told her to "get in the car." She got in the back seat and we began driving home. I was scolding her, talking a mile a minute about how bad she was, how worried we had been, etc., etc. etc. when she suddenly leaned over the back seat and burped in my ear. It was too funny and I just dissolved into laughter. That was the first and last time that she ever left her yard (except to say "Hi" to the pre-school kids).

We returned home to Ohio when Princess was two years old. Until we could get on our feet, we lived in the basement apartment of my mother and dad's home. Princess took the trip home very well, spending most of her time sleeping in the back seat. We would stop at a motel and book a room usually late at night and then just take her in. She was so good and quiet that they never knew we had a dog in the room.

During this time my parents had a parakeet named Pete. He loved to torment Princess by calling "here kitty kitty" and then whistling like when you call a dog. She would come over to the cage and stand looking at him as if to say, "well, what do you want?" He would wait until she stuck her face up close to the bars and then he would peck her nose. She never did figure out what he was all about and always came when he called the kitty.

Pete had a girlfriend (whose name I can't remember). She was a pretty blue parakeet who liked to take baths. They had one of those bathtubs that you connect to the side of the cage. She would get in there and attempt to flap around and get a bath but Pete would have none of it. He would get her by the tail and pull her backwards out of the bathtub. The only way the female ever got her bath was if we took Pete out of the cage.

11

"Hey, This White Stuff Is Fun!"

A few days after we moved back to Ohio it began to snow. The first time we let Princess out in it she ran out, skidded to a stop, stuck her nose deep in the snow, flipped it up in the air and then started running around and jumping like a nut. She loved it!! While I was grumbling about the snow, my florida-born baby was having a great time playing in the white stuff.

She never tired of it. Even as she got older and more arthritic, she still asked to go for a walk when it was snowing so she could enjoy the stuff. It always brought out the puppy in her and made her want to play.

She liked to have snowballs thrown at her. She would try to catch them and was mystified when they broke into pieces in her mouth. She would also get down in the puppy play position with head down and butt up and dare you to kick snow at her. She would get snow all over her face and then jump and shake until it all came off. Then she'd come back for more. I always ended these play sessions long before she was ready to - I hated snow!

Soon Princess and I parted company with our Air Force guy and moved into our own duplex. There were a lot of kids on the street and she was in her glory. She used to sit outside at the curb and watch them play baseball. She knew she was not allowed in the street so she would wait patiently. Inevitably the ball would come up on the curb and she would grab it and run away, hoping they would chase her. From inside I would hear, "oh no, she's got the ball again." She never tired of this game but the kids did and soon the ball game would be over.

The mailman had to come into a vestibule to put mail in the mailboxes of the two tenants. He would always leave a dog biscuit in the mailbox for Princess and one for the dog next door. If I wasn't home when he came she would have to wait, but the minute I walked in the door she would start going to the front door and barking - she wanted me to get that mail!

Once shortly after Princess and I had moved into the duplex and gone "on our own," I received a five-pound box of candy from a friend on Valentine's Day. I had been sick with the flu and hadn't touched any of the candy but had left it on the end table in the living room. I returned home one evening and found what looked like dog doo doo all over the house. Closer inspection proved it to be vomited chocolate candy. There were little pieces of foil where "someone" had eaten each piece whole, paper and all. It was a mystery at first, because the box of candy appeared to be untouched. Since Princess and I lived alone I had to surmise that even though the lid was firmly on the box, she had somehow lifted up the lid, gotten the candy and then let the lid back down.

At the time I thought it was funny, although I felt bad for her having to be sick like that. Now, it scares me to death to think of it knowing that chocolate is so toxic for dogs!

13

Princess and I found a house on the same street as my sister and her family in 1973 and moved there. One of my sister's cats had just had a litter of kittens and I spent lots of time over there watching them play. There was one particular kitten in the litter, a long-haired white cat with gray patches. I loved to watch it play. The other kittens would be sleeping and this one would be so tired that it would be leaning against the wall with eyes closed instead of curled up with the others. It must have been afraid it would miss something because even when leaning against the wall if their dog Lady would go by, it would leap on the dog and then run away. It had a lot of personality and I started thinking about maybe adopting it but only if it were a female. We finally took the kittens to the vet for checkups and to determine sexes. Alas, my kitten turned out to be a male. Oh well, I told my sister, I don't want a male cat, but in a couple of weeks when she warned me that someone else was going to take him, I panicked and changed my mind. It started another chapter for Princess and me.

Beauregard, or Boo Boo as I came to call him, was a very active, mischievous kitten. He was into everything and considered himself the ruler of the house. He established this dynasty with Princess and never relinquished his "Top Dog" status to anyone. Princess accepted his antics and allowed him to act out all his fantasies. If she were laying down, he would first attack her paws and then try to jump on her head. She would very patiently move each paw away from him and when he jumped for her head she would move it out of the way. If she were walking, he would attack her tail and try to hang from it. Or he would wait on the other side of a door and when she passed through he would leap out (all two pounds of him) with paws upraised as if to pounce on her. She would just ignore him and keep going. If he became too boisterous for her, she would just go into another room.

14

One of my Christmas passions was a live Christmas tree. I had always had one and planned to continue the tradition. Beauregard changed all that. Our first Christmas together I had put up the tree and gone to bed. I was awakened by a rustling, jingling noise and got up and went into the living room. With the light from the street light outside shining into the room, I saw two yellow eyes staring out at me from my Christmas tree. When I turned on the light, I discovered he was hanging, upside down from the trunk of the tree. I extricated him from that and took him into the bedroom with me.

The next day when I returned home from work, my Christmas tree was overturned on the floor. Many glass ornaments were broken and the water was spilled on the carpet. This was not going to work. I redid the tree and put sandbags around the tree holder to weight it down. During the night I awoke several times to rustling and jingling but didn't get up.

The next evening I returned home again from work to find the Christmas tree on the floor again with more ornaments broken and another wet carpet. I was losing my sense of humor. I moved the tree over in front of the window and used some fishing line to tie it to the window handle. During the night the usual jingling, tinkling sounds came from the living room.

Next evening I found the tree upright but missing about 90% of its trimmings. He had systematically removed every piece of tinsel, every ornament, every bit of garland that he could reach. He, of course, was sitting innocently amongst the branches.

It became a nightly ritual. I returned home and re-trimmed the tree while he sat watching me. After two years I succumbed to the frustration and purchased an artificial tree. This appeared to satisfy Beauregard because he never tried to 'de-trim' or climb the artificial tree but would only sometimes lay underneath it and swat at low hanging ornaments.

15

"Hey Doc, I Need Some Help Here!"

When Beauregard was four months old and weighed about 10 pounds, he began lifting his leg on the furniture to mark his territory. I called the vet and wanted to make an appointment to have him neutered. They said that he was too young and doc wouldn't do it until he was at least six months old.

Another week went by and his behavior worsened. He now decided not to use the litter box at all. I called the vet again and said "I need some help here!" They said to bring him in and doc would look at him. It was a ploy to placate me, I'm sure, since I was sounding so desperate on the phone. When I walked into the office with this huge four months old cat they said "that's Beauregard? No problem we'll do him."

The neutering solved the aggressive territory marking and he returned to his normal, inquisitive self, although I don't think he ever forgave me for destroying his manhood.

Beauregard's Big Adventure

Beauregard was always curious when Princess went outside and I constantly had to push him back to keep him from going out the door. Since he was declawed, I wanted to keep him safe indoors. One winter evening he exasperated me trying to get out, so I picked him up and threw him out the door into about a foot of snow. It was quite comical to see him stiffen his legs and try to walk on top of the snow back into the house. That seemed to satisfy his curiosity and he stopped trying to go out the door with Princess.

Years later after I had remarried and we had purchased a house with two acres of land, Boo Boo somehow slipped out the back door while we were letting the dogs out and didn't "slip back in" when they came in. We hadn't missed him and were sitting in the family room watching TV when someone knocked on the front door. My husband went to the door and it was Beauregard. He had apparently waited at the back door and when we didn't return he came around front and had to bear the indignity of knocking to be let in.

Frank was afraid to yell at him to "get in here" for fear he would run away, so he calmly looked at Boo Boo and said, "hi, would you like to come in?" Beauregard entered regally and stalked into the family room, his displeasure evident.

17

Look Out For That Skunk.................. Oh No!

Spring arrived in Ohio, and Princess went outside in my folk's backyard to take a walk and do whatever it is dogs do when they do it. All we heard was "bark, bark" then came the unmistakable smell of skunk. Poor Princess, she had found  something to play with, that didn't want to play. She was very dejected and in considerable pain when we got to her. The skunk had sprayed directly into her eyes. After flushing her eyes out with water, we tackled the chore of washing her in tomato juice.

The worst part was that this was to have been her final trip outside before bedtime. By now it was midnight and we certainly were not in the mood to give the dog a tomato juice bath.

She was very sheepish throughout this bathing procedure and really didn't want to talk about it. We finished drying her (the white fur still showing a slight pinkish cast from the tomato juice) and then took her inside.

Let's face it, tomato juice really doesn't do the trick. It lessens the smell but only time will erase the awful reminder of a "deadly" encounter. So for the next couple of weeks the house had the distinct aroma of skunk.

Experience was not the best teacher in this little drama. Princess had two more meetings with skunks and sorry to say she came out on the short end every time.

18

When I left my parents home at age 19 to "be on my own," I put off the tempting idea of obtaining a pet until I had what I considered a proper place to have a pet. Snoopy did not wait for me to decide to have a pet, she chose me.

I was living in an apartment on the second floor of a house. One evening when I came in from work, I discovered a very pretty cat sitting on the sidewalk by my door. She was a gray calico with orange patches. I stooped to pet her and then went in. For the next few days she was outside when I got home and seemed to be waiting for me, so the next night I stopped and bought some cat food. When I got home, she was indeed waiting so I invited her to come upstairs for dinner. She happily complied. After dinner she stayed long enough to be polite and then meowed at the door to leave.

We repeated this procedure for a couple of weeks and after having a few good meals it was apparent that she was pregnant. I felt good about feeding her when she was going to have kittens at any time.

One evening when I came home Snoopy (by this time I had named her) wasn't there. I was not overly concerned but thought that she might have had her litter. The next evening, same thing, no Snoopy. I was beginning to get a little nervous by the third evening but didn't know what I could do. I was sitting on the couch watching TV when something moved outside my window. It scared the daylights out of me since I was on the second floor, but went over to the window to see what it was.

Snoopy stood on the roof peering in the window waiting for me to open it. I thought, "what a smart cat!" To get to this window she had to climb a tree on the other side of the house, go over the roof to the opposite side of the house to my window. Anyway, she had figured it out and found me. She was very thin and it was evident that she had already had the kittens. I fed her and then let her go back out.

I Find The Kittens

Each night after the kittens were born, Snoopy would come to the window to be fed. I let her leave by way of the window because it seemed convenient for both of us. After she left, I would go downstairs and try to see where she went, because I wanted to find her kittens. She would elude me every time. This went on for a couple of weeks.

Finally I realized if I was going to find the kittens I would have to make her go out the door and then follow her.

She was too smart for me and just disappeared. So the next time I went the other way around the house and waited to see where she would go. She carefully looked each way to make sure no one was watching and then slipped through the bushes into the basement window gutter. I slowly parted the bushes and there they were, five beautiful, fluffy, kittens about three weeks old.

I asked for, and received, permission to pick one of them up. She watched me closely but didn't seem alarmed. I told her we were going to have to bring them upstairs so nothing would happen to them. She acquiesced. I took them upstairs and made a bed for them under the end table with some old blankets and towels. She didn't like that spot and moved them into a quiet corner in the dining room.

20

Snoopy And I Disagree On Training Methods

Snoopy spent the day inside the apartment now while I was at work caring for the kittens. When I came home, she would go to the window and ask to go out. She would go out for a few hours and then come back to stay with the kittens at night.

One evening I let her out and she hadn't returned by midnight. I was tired and decided to go to bed and leave the window open enough for her to get in.

Before I had fallen asleep I heard her come in. Something told me to get up and check. I went into the living room in my bare feet and stepped on something wet. I turned on the light to find I had stepped on a dead baby bird that Snoopy had brought home for dinner for the children. She was quite insulted that I wouldn't let her have it, and we started a new policy. If she wasn't home by the time I went to bed then she could either stay outside or knock on the window. Over the course of raising these kittens she did both.

21

Snoopy Goes Traveling

My Air Force husband completed his basic training in Texas and then after we were married he was sent to Denver for school. Snoopy accompanied us and did pretty well in the car until we got to Kansas. It was fall and everything was dry and bleak. The tumbleweed was blowing across the plains and would blow up on the road, hitting the car and bursting into a million pieces.

She had a hard time dealing with the tumbleweed and spent the entire trip through Kansas underneath the front seat. Colorado went smoothly for her but when we went on to Florida she didn't adjust quite as well.

In Florida there are large cockroaches called palmetto bugs. They are about three or four inches long and totally disgusting. They can flatten themselves out and slip under the door. They like damp, dark places and unless you have a "bug man" you will have them in your house.

We couldn't afford "the bug man," so we lived with them. Snoopy however, never adjusted to them. She would not kill them, but she would stun them and then come and get me to kill them for her.

We had very tame gray squirrels outside our first Florida cottage that were used to being fed by my landlord. He taught me to feed them raw peanuts and since there was a small hole in my screen door they soon learned to climb up there and chatter to get a peanut. Snoopy was very traumatized by the squirrels climbing up the screen and would sometimes leap against the screen door at them. They were less than alarmed by this and sometimes Snoopy and a squirrel would end up eyeball to eyeball hanging on the screen door.

She was with us for a couple of years in Florida, but while I was on a trip home to Ohio my husband accidently let her get out of the house and she was never seen again. I believe she returned to the wild and was happy.

My nephew David was three years old the first time my sister and brother-in-law visited us in Panama City. He was a good kid but we worked hard trying to find enough things to keep him occupied. I had a three-pound coffee can full of peanuts and showed David how to feed the squirrels through the hole in the screen. I wasn't worried because the hole was small and the squirrels were used to being fed through there and they were very tame.

One morning we all got up and found that David had been up for hours, feeding the squirrels peanuts. The whole three pound can was empty and the squirrels were absolutely sated. They were busy burying nuts because they didn't know what else to do with them. They sort of waddled around for a few days and didn't ask for any peanuts. My guess is that they buried enough for five or six winters, and it doesn't even get cold there!

Apples & Tommy

During an Explorer Scout seminar at Philmont Boy Scout Ranch in New Mexico we had the opportunity to go horseback riding.

Frank had never been on a horse, but I assured him that these horses were trail horses and really didn't care whether you could ride or not. They followed each other on the trail and virtually ignored their rider.

We were given instructions, our horse assignments and we all saddled up in the paddock. I was assigned "Tommy" while Frank got "Apples." Tommy didn't wait for direction, as soon as I was mounted he started out of the paddock, falling into line behind the other horses.

Frank was three horses behind me and as we moved onto the trail I noticed that after Frank's horse there was a gap of about 25 feet before the next horse. That seemed odd to me since the others stayed one right behind the other. I could see Frank laughing hysterically and didn't learn what was so funny until we took our halfway break.

It seems that "Apples" had some sort of allergy. He would take two steps, sneeze and then loudly and very fragrantly pass gas. The other horses and especially the other riders wanted to stay far behind, or preferably ahead of, Apples.

Frank was afraid that when Apples did both the sneezing and the flatulence at the same time, that the horse was going to explode and he feared for his life.

On the trip back I had more to concern myself with than Apples' tricks. It seemed that Tommy didn't like water and the back trail had three spots where we had to cross the stream. It was all I could do to keep Tommy from tossing me in the water every time we slid down the bank to cross the stream. It got so bad that I was talking to him; "come on Tommy, I don't like the water any more than you do, let's just get across this together, O.K?" He wasn't impressed.

Once we got back on the main trail, all the horses knew it was almost over. They began trotting to get back to the barn quickly. This was my first horseback ride in many years and my poor old body was pretty sore. What I did not need was to trot back to the paddock. My whole concentration was now on keeping Tommy at a walk.

All in all it was a nice ride in beautiful, breathtaking New Mexico country.

The Cat With No Meow

When Princess was about six months old and we were living in the trailer, I found a little abandoned orange kitten at the Laundromat. I brought it home and it remained with us, staying mostly outside but coming in during the bad weather. Snoopy didn't seem to mind, she just ignored it.

We just called her "Kitty" and she was quite sweet. I was working second shift at the hospital and when I would get home from work she would be waiting outside the trailer door for me so I could bring her in to eat.

One evening she wasn't there and it worried me enough to look for her. I found her lying beside the trailer and took her inside. She was dirty and was injured. There was no blood but she couldn't walk.

We called the vet and he met us at the office. He checked her over and said it looked as thought she had been hit by a car. He wasn't too optimistic but suggested that we leave her overnight and we would see what developed.

Next day he phoned and said she was doing pretty well. She still couldn't walk but was alert and eating. He said if she continued to improve we could take her home the next day.

The next morning I called and he said "come and get her." When I got there, he told me she still couldn't walk but that he expected she would get her equilibrium back within a few days. He explained she probably had a slight concussion.

 Kitty became an inside cat for the time being. We gave her a nice comfortable box and kept her warm and fed. She improved rapidly and learned to walk while leaning up against the wall to keep from falling over. As her equilibrium improved she was able to walk without the aid of

26

the wall and soon was venturing outside again. She was never really the same, however, and never regained her "meow." She would look at me and say "ack."

One night I returned home from work and she wasn't at the door. I got really worried and started calling her. I heard the distinct "ack" coming from the woods outside the back fence. I went out there with a flashlight and kept calling her. She kept answering and I finally located her high up in a pine tree, at least 25 feet. I called her and said "come down," so she did - she just jumped. I shined my flashlight on the ground expecting to see a smashed cat but she was walking toward me. I guess it's true - they do have nine lives.

I subsequently found her a nice home with a retired couple so I didn't have to worry about her other seven lives.

The Story Of Daniel

Princess and I spent a year's lease living in an apartment on the second floor. The apartment was really nice and quite large, but I never got used to the noise of other people and the inconvenience of having to take Princess down two flights of stairs several times a day.

On one of our jaunts outside we found a little kitten that couldn't have been more than three weeks old. He was all alone, without a mom. I checked around in the woods and left him alone for a couple of hours hoping that she would come back. He was very weak and couldn't stand up on his own.

It looked like the Mother cat had met with misfortune or had abandoned him. I couldn't leave him outside to fend for himself and it was obvious that he needed food badly.

I brought him upstairs and warmed some milk which I fed him with an eyedropper. Before long he started to come around and was able to stand by himself.

He was too young to be on his own and I had a brilliant idea! My sister's mama cat had just had a litter of kittens. Maybe she would accept this little orphan and feed him.

Princess and I took the little kitten over to my sister's and placed him in the box with the other kittens. At first the mama was upset and hissed at the kitten, but she soon realized that he was not a threat to her babies and was just a baby himself. She let him nurse and accepted him into her family.

The one remaining stumbling block would be my brother-in-law. He was not happy that the cat had just had another litter and would not be happy to accept this orphan.

My sister and I decided that since there were already five kittens, perhaps he wouldn't notice the sixth. He came in from work and was soon relaxing on the couch in the family room.

28

The kittens were frolicking on the floor and he was watching them.

Suddenly he got a puzzled look on his face and started counting the kittens. "Wait a minute," he said, "there were only five of these little beggars yesterday. What's going on?" We had to tell him and thought he was going to have a fit, but he must have felt sorry for the kitten because he let him stay.

After the kittens were big enough to adopt out, my sister's family decided to keep the orphaned kitten and named him Daniel. He was beautiful; black with white paws, a white chest and a white spot on his nose. He was an extraordinary kitten with a lot of personality. He acted as though he was grateful that we had saved him from starvation or something worse. Whenever any of the family picked him up when he didn't want to be bothered, even if it were the smallest child, he never scratched or bit any of us. If he wanted down he would just meow. To other cats and other animals he was a fierce tomcat but to all of us he was just "Daniel" a real pussycat.

Once during the time of Daniel, I had a broken left wrist (I'm left-handed). Pat had asked me to come over for dinner since I was so pathetic without my left hand.

She had pork chops for dinner and as I was struggling to cut my food and begin to eat, a little black and white paw came up from under the table and grabbed for my pork chop.

Quick fork stabbing on my part was the only thing that saved my pork chop from being part of Daniel's dinner that night. I guess he figured he would pick on the weakest member of the family, the crippled one with the cast.

The Calico Fraidy Cat

Before I got Beauregard, I had rented a house in Mentor, Ohio near the lake. It was a cottage, really, on a concrete slab. Before long Princess and I realized we had mice.

Not being the kind of person who could set a trap and then dispose of bodies and not wanting poison in the house because of Princess, I decided to "borrow" a cat from my sister to chase away the mice. She had a calico cat about a year old and let me borrow her for a while, with no guarantees. What a joke! This cat was so afraid of Princess and I guess of me too that she went into the bathroom, got on the top shelf of the linen closet and stayed there.

In order to keep her from starving, I had to put food in the bathroom and close the door. After a couple of hours I would look in and the food would be eaten, but the cat would be back on the top shelf of the linen closet. This went on for about a week and I decided I'd better return this cat before she had a nervous breakdown.

Her actual presence in the house must have convinced the mice to vacate, but if one of them had come near her, I'm sure the calico cat would have found an even higher place to hide.

I returned her to her owner who reminded me (with a smile) that she hadn't been lent out with any promises. I guess she knew some things about this cat that she neglected to tell me.

When Princess and I looked at the "mouse" cottage, I was impressed with the fact that it had a fenced-in yard. I thought it would be great because I could leave Princess outside during the day while I was at work, a luxury I hadn't had in the apartment.

I purchased a chain bicycle lock that I could put around the gate to keep anyone from opening it, (I was well acquainted with little people who wanted to see "Lassie"). There was a covered patio and I left the door to the garage open so she could go in and out of there too.

It was the ideal situation for both of us. I felt good because she wasn't cooped up and she really loved being outside again.

One evening after I got home from work and Princess was still outside, I saw a police car pull into the driveway. The officer got out of his car and walked toward the back yard.

I went out the back door and he was talking to Princess over the fence and she was just wagging her tail. I asked if I could help him with something and he said that the police department had received a complaint about Princess barking. It seems there was a 'day sleeper' on the street behind us and Princess was keeping him up.

I said, "my dog? no way. She doesn't bark." He said that he tended to agree with me since he had walked up the driveway and she hadn't barked at him, nor did she bark when he got out of his car.

He didn't know what I knew. There were <u>squirrels</u> in the yard, the one thing Princess couldn't resist barking at. I knew instantly that the complaint was valid, but decided to let him dismiss it as a crank call.

I told him that I was not going to restrict my dog to the inside since the fenced-in yard was the main reason I had rented this house. I told him that they had to be mistaken, it couldn't be my dog that was barking.

He left and I had a long talk with Princess. I explained that she was going to have to be quiet when she was outside or I was going to be forced to keep her inside while I was gone. Like "Lassie" she listened to every word and must have understood because there were no further complaints. But now my dog had a record!

The Final Summer

Princess was delighted when Frank and I were married. She had another human who loved her and she also had a new yard. We had two and a half acres bordered on one side by woods.

Our wonderful neighbor, Marian, who also had two and a half acres bordered on the opposite side also by woods, loved Princess and allowed her to roam freely in her yard too. Wow, five acres! A real paradise for a dog like Princess.

That was June of 1978 and Princess enjoyed that summer and fall but began to suffer some health problems in the winter. She was now 12 years old and had some problems with failing kidneys and arthritis, common ailments with collies after age 10.

In the summer of 1979 we decided not to vacation away so that we would not have to kennel Princess. We rented a cottage on the lake not far from our home and spent a week there.

Princess was in her glory. We put a mattress from one of the cots on the floor next to the bed and covered it with blankets and rugs so she wouldn't have to sleep on the cold, bare floor.
I would cover her with a throw rug and she would sleep, without moving or disturbing her 'blanket' all night long. It was a great vacation and as it turned out we were right to not leave her. Princess died August 31, 1979.

The loss of Princess was very hard on me. She was my companion, my best friend and my confidant through some of the worst times of my life. I found that I was crying all the time. I would come home from work, there would be no Princess to meet me and I would start crying again.

Beauregard was quite affected by her loss too. He would go to the back door, put his paws up on the screen and look out. He would meow at me insistently as if to say "let her in!" After a couple of weeks he seemed to accept that she was gone but it took a little longer for me.

Someone at work told me about a collie that a breeder had that they wanted to get rid of. It seems that this 3-year-old collie female had never had a heat period and thus was 'useless' to this breeder. She had stated that if she couldn't find a home for this dog she was going to have it put to sleep.

Frank suggested that we go look at the dog because I imagine he was really sick of me crying all the time. Princess and Beauregard had been his first experience with pets and I think he also wanted to erase the bad memory of losing one.

I told Frank that I wouldn't automatically take this dog just because she was a collie. I jawed all the way over there about how I knew about collies and I would know if this one had a good temperament or not and I would make up my mind after I saw the dog whether or not to take her.

We got over there and the breeder said she had the dog on the porch and would get her for us. She opened the door, I crouched down and this beautiful, mahogany sable collie walked into my arms and put her head on my shoulder. I said "we'll take her." Frank was too nice to point out about how I knew about collies and this wasn't automatic, etc., etc., etc.

They had named her 'Pepino', a cute name for a Chihuahua, but a perfectly awful name for a collie. She didn't appear to even recognize the name, so we changed her name to 'Randi' on the way home.

We brought her in the back door to get her used to that. I never let my animals use the front door unless they are on a leash and are going with me in the car. This keeps them from going in the front yard and keeps them away from the street. Beauregard was sitting on the screened-in porch when we brought her in and she walked right past him. He continued to wash his paws for a minute and then you could almost see it click in his mind. His head snapped around and he came after Randi and hissed at her. I told him to forget it, he had already blown it, she was in.

They too became great friends and he pretended to dominate her while she pretended to allow it. He again had to grieve the loss of a friend when we lost her in 1988 at age 13.

Randi was a wonderful dog with a lot of problems. Since she was three years old when we got her, a lot of her conditioning had already happened. They had apparently tormented her with the lawn mower because she hated it and would bark and charge it every time. She was very timid and I suspected she was not treated very well in her first home.

When we brought her home she was very scared and I decided to take a couple of days off work and be with her. She hadn't spent any time in the house and therefore was not house trained. She followed me around everywhere and during those two days I trained her to go outside and I guess we really bonded. From the time that we first got her she was always very close to me.

She had never seen TV and that was really funny. Whenever the doorbell would ring on TV, she would run to the door and bark. People would be talking on a TV show and she would stare at the screen, listen and cock her head trying to understand what they were saying.

Heartworm!!

We made an appointment at our vet's soon after we brought Randi home to have her checked out. He said he thought she was older than three years because her teeth were loaded with tarter, but said that it could be a result of poor quality food.

As almost an afterthought, due to the fact that heartworm had not been prevalent in our town, he decided to do the heartworm blood test. Before I even got back home, the phone was ringing.

She had heartworm and we discussed the treatment. She would have to take medication for three weeks to kill the active worms and then additional medication to kill the micro filaria, or eggs.

I notified the breeder that we had gotten Randi from of the heartworm, but even though she had several litters of puppies that she was selling and shipping to various parts of the country she wasn't concerned. She only wanted to know if I had put the dog to sleep. I replied, "no, we're going to treat the heartworm." She replied that it was very expensive treatment. I assured her that it didn't matter, we would have the dog treated.

The next day I picked up the medication and began administering it as directed. She became violently ill, throwing up several times. I called the vet and he said to give her another dose at the appointed time to see if it was indeed the medication that was making her sick. It was.

He prescribed a different medication with the same result. She was violently ill, throwing up the purple medication, but would ask to go out every time and never soiled the carpet. Doc said to give her some Pepto Bismol but that also came up. When nothing would work, Doc had me meet him at the office (it was 1:00 in the morning). He gave her a shot of something to stop the vomiting and nausea and we sat in the waiting room chatting while we watched for the medication to take affect.

When she finally curled up to go to sleep, we knew she was going to be O.K.

I got out my checkbook to pay for this emergency treatment but Doc said "no charge." I protested that this was above and beyond the call of duty, it was 2:00 in the morning! He stated that he could not in clear conscience charge for easing the dog's illness that was caused by medication he had prescribed. He was adamant. He wouldn't accept payment.

Subsequently she had to have shots, every day for two weeks and learned to hate going to the vet's office. Doc was wonderful with her and she always loved him, even though she knew a shot was imminent. The medicine cured the heartworm, but we were warned that the damage to the heart would probably shorten her life.

There is nothing else I can say about the conduct of both my vet and the breeder that we got Randi from. I cannot name the breeder publicly for fear of a lawsuit and my vet would be embarrassed by the notoriety, but if you live in the Northeastern Ohio area and want a wonderful, caring, vet - call me, (I'm in the phone book) - I'll tell you.

All in all, I'm very glad we got Randi. She was a wonderful pet and we saved her from heaven only knows what. As we had been warned about the heart damage, we expected that the heartworm disease would shorten her life, but she fooled all of us and lived a quite average collie life cycle.

Randi And Fireworks

We got Randi in September so she had 10 months to adjust before the July 4th Holiday rolled around.

She was doing pretty well, she had accepted the TV, she was great pals with Beauregard and she had discovered the cold water supply (known to most of us as the toilet).

We had to be out performing on July 4th (we have a band but that's another story, another book, another time). We never dreamed that Randi would be so traumatized by the sounds of firecrackers but then we weren't aware that our neighbors on the other side had great fun shooting off firecrackers and shooting rockets into our backyard while we weren't home.

We came home to find that Randi had disappeared. Now it's a little hard for a 50-pound dog to disappear, but we searched the house and couldn't find her. I called her and called her and was getting really scared when I spotted her in the family room - under the TV! It is a floor model Zenith with no more than a 12-inch clearance between the bottom of the cabinet and the floor, but she was so scared that she had somehow crawled under there. We had to pick up and move the TV to get her out. She never got over that fear of loud noises. I guess they must have tormented her with more than lawn mowers.

38

We Get A Puppy

When Randi was seven and had been with us for four years, we decided to get a puppy. I didn't want to have my heart ripped totally out when this dog left us. I figured that if we got another dog every five years or so, we would always have at least one to lessen the grief. Nothing takes away the devastation when you lose a beloved pet, but if you have other pets it helps.

We found a good breeder (not the one where we got Randi!!) and went out to see the puppies. The lady, Kitty, took us out to see the kennels. They were immaculate. She asked if we wanted to see the parents and we said yes.

The puppies mother was a very pretty tri-color, but when she opened the cage to let the father out I gasped. He was the biggest and most beautiful sable collie I had ever seen.

We talked in her kitchen while the puppies played and we decided to purchase one of the gorgeous females. She was already three months old so we could take her right away. She cried all the way to our house and broke my heart for taking her away from her mom.

As soon as we brought the puppy in the house she stopped crying because she had spotted Randi. They bonded instantly and Randi became the surrogate mother to the new puppy, Sabra.

We took the new puppy to the vet's as soon as we got her, as was our practice, to be checked out and to get all the puppy shots. Doc said she was going to be big. I commented that I had thought so too because of the size of her paws. He said no, he was looking at the size of her head. She grew to 78 and a half pounds by the time she was two. It seemed as though Sabra was never a puppy - she just grew so quickly.

Sabra My Soulmate

Sabra, oh how do I describe Sabra? This dog, of all my wonderful dogs, touched something in me like no pet before her or since. She was beautiful, loyal, with an abundance of the inherent intelligence of her breed. She was truly the smartest dog I've ever seen. If I wanted to teach her something I only had to show her once. Lassie had nothing on this dog.

She stayed in constant contact with me, watching me and listening to everything I said just in case I was talking to her. Wherever I was in the house, she would be there too. If I went outside and didn't take her, she would stand at the door and wait for me to return. She had the gentlest, sweetest temperament of all my girls. She tried desperately to talk. She made noises that sounded almost like words. Whenever you would ask her a question like, "what's the matter?", she would try to tell you. She was truly my soulmate.

When Sabra was just six months old, she was walking with me in the back yard. It was March with still a good bit of snow on the ground. There was a frozen pool of water near the property line that was perhaps four or five inches deep. I walked on it and there was a loud crack as the ice broke. Sabra grabbed my wrist in her mouth and pulled me off the ice. I was laughing because it was only a puddle, but when I thought about it I was pretty impressed. She didn't know it was only four inches deep. For all she knew, she was saving me from breaking through the ice and drowning. All this intelligence from a six-month-old puppy.

When she was older, she had a unique way of getting us up in the morning. She would walk beside the bed and slam her body into the side of the mattress. She could get about three good slams on each side. She would do this until we woke up (which didn't take very long - when a 78-pound dog slamsherself into the side of the bed it makes the bed shake like an earthquake!!) Very effective - who needs an alarm clock?

Randi & Sabra Go Exploring

Randi truly acted the 'mom' for Sabra, teaching her about "going" outside and all the social skills she needed to be a good pet. They slept close together, usually back-to-back and as a general rule, where you saw one you saw the other. Sabra followed her everywhere outside, too, and I never worried about them. Randi loved us passionately and had no desire to go anywhere. I knew Sabra was safe with her.

One afternoon they had gone outside and enough time had elapsed that I felt they should have come back. I went outside looking for them and couldn't find them anywhere. Panic set in. You think all kinds of crazy things - like someone has kidnaped them. I put on my boots, (it was spring and the ground was still muddy) and went looking for them. Frank got in the car to drive over to the housing development that was on the other side of the woods which bordered Marian's property.

Frank found them walking along one of the streets in the development and called them to get in the car. They jumped in and enjoyed the ride home. Their enjoyment ended when they got home and I began to scold them. I explained all the reasons why they shouldn't leave the yard and told them in no uncertain terms that I would not permit it. They both listened politely and certainly appeared to understand.

Randi continued to slip through the woods into the housing development, several more times over the next few years, but Sabra never again left the yard. The way I would know that Randi had gone was Sabra would be standing at the point where Randi went into the woods, for all I knew trying to get her to come back. I could almost imagine the conversation that could have passed between them; Randi saying "come on Sab, let's go over to the housing development and see what's over there." Sabra saying, "no way, our mom told us never to leave the yard. You go if you want to, but I'm not going." Sabra would follow Randi anywhere so long as it didn't require disappointing her humans by disobeying them and leaving the yard.

When I met and fell in love with Frank, I soon learned that he had never had a pet. Even as a child he wasn't allowed a dog, or a cat or anything. Instinctively I knew not to bring both Princess and Beauregard to his house to visit at the same time.

I often brought Princess with me as she was no trouble and Frank predictably fell in love with her. But somehow I forgot to mention that I also had a cat.

Frank and I went away for a weekend and took Princess with us. Before we left, I went home and made sure Beauregard had plenty of food and water and that his box was clean. I knew he would be O.K. for two days. Little did I know that he would make me pay for this little weekend away!!

When we got home Sunday evening and Frank dropped us off, I immediately looked for Beauregard to check on him. He was nowhere to be found. "Oh oh" I said. "He must be mad." Mad would probably be a mild description of what I encountered when I went in the spare room.

Beauregard was sitting on top of a box of Christmas decorations with his flea collar (still buckled around his neck) in his mouth. He had somehow gotten it into his mouth (trying to take it off, I guess) and it was jammed there forcing his mouth wide open. Obviously he couldn't eat or drink with that thing jammed in there like that. I quickly cut it off him and he went instantly to the water dish and drank for a long time. Now I had to live with the guilt of having left him alone. Maybe he had been that way all weekend! How could I have been so irresponsible?

He would not talk to me. He would not look at me. He would not get on my lap (and this was the same cat who stayed glued to me whenever I was seated). I knew I was in trouble. He never really got over being mad at me and after Frank and I were married he made himself Frank's cat. He still loved me and would sit on my lap occasionally, but he preferred Frank.

Of all my animals I guess I have the most Beauregard stories to tell. He seemed to be always either getting into something he wasn't supposed to be in, or complaining about something or causing some kind of commotion.

I came home from work one evening tired, burned out, and ready to relax and watch some TV. I fixed something to eat and sat down in the living room to enjoy the news and eat my dinner.

Much rustling began coming from the chimney along with puffs of soot. Was Santa about to visit me in March? Oh no, it was Mr. Beauregard trying to climb up the inside of the chimney.

Dinner abandoned, I went over to the fireplace and tried to see how I could extricate him from this latest mess. Very reminiscent of the Christmas tree scene, he was hanging upside down inside the chimney. All I could see was his head with two big yellow eyes looking out of a black face.

I managed to pull him out of there and what a mess! He was covered in greasy soot. He had to be taken immediately to the bathroom for a bath.

Now Beauregard liked a bath about as much as he liked taking medicine (a subject yet to be covered). For the next two hours we fought through the soaping, rinsing, more soaping more rinsing and drying procedures. Of course no matter how well you dried him it was never good enough. He always would spend the next hour indignantly washing himself. And, needless to say, he wouldn't speak to me for days.

Now I had to figure out a way to keep him out of the fireplace chimney. The purchase of a fireplace screen solved the problem, but he would, could and did find more things with which to make my life more interesting.

Beauregard Watches TV

When he wasn't climbing up the
chimney, Beauregard like to watch TV.
His version was a little different from
ours, however. He would lay on top of
the TV with front paws and head
hanging over, watching what was going
on. If there was something moving, like
a car driving along, or a horse galloping across the screen, he
would try to catch it. I got used to watching TV with the top
part of the screen covered by batting paws.

It was most entertaining to watch him when he got so involved
in batting at something that he fell off the TV. Of course he
always landed on his feet and to maintain his dignity he would
act as though that was what he wanted to do all along. The
scratches are still there on the top of the console TV, a lasting
reminder of Beauregard.

Beauregard was always very curious about everything. This is
a cat trait, I know, but he seemed to have an overabundance of
curiosity. No matter what I was doing, I could count of Boo
Boo being right beside me, checking everything out and
sticking his nose in where it really didn't belong. Like the
peanut butter cookie instance . . .

I was making peanut butter cookies and he just wouldn't leave
me alone. He was trying to get up on the counter; meowing and
getting in front of my legs so that I almost tripped over him
every time I turned. I finally gave him a taste of the peanut
butter, a round ball about 1/4 inch thick. He began to chew it
and then, of course, it got stuck to the roof of his mouth.

He stuck his paw inside his mouth trying to paw the peanut
butter off the roof. It took him several minutes to get it unstuck
and this seemed to satisfy his curiosity about the baking.
Whenever I got the best of him like this, he would go away and
leave me alone for a little while. Probably plotting his next
bedevilment.

45

Beauregard Takes A Swim

Beauregard always came into the bathroom when I was taking a bath. He seemed fascinated with the bathtub - filled with the dreaded water. One of our little rented houses had an old fashioned claw foot bathtub. He loved to get up on the edge while I bathing and walk all around. Well, you've seen this part coming, I'm sure - on one occasion he fell in.

It was the quickest dip in history. I believe he may have had divine guidance for it looked like he walked on water. No sooner did his body touch the water than he shot straight up and out of the tub.

When I got out and got a towel to dry him, the only part of him that was wet was his tail and one back leg. So what I thought I had seen was really true. He really got out of there quickly!!

Again, he was pretty smart - he didn't 'walk the line' again, just sat in the bathroom and watched.

Chickens

It took a long time for me to find out why I'm afraid of chickens. It seemed quite unreasonable. Chickens don't normally strike fear into the hearts of man. One rarely sees a horror movie with the starring role being a monster chicken. So it remained a mystery for a long time.

All I could recall was spending summers on the farm when I was nine, 10 and 11 and having to do chores. Since I was a 'city girl' they figured a good chore for me would be to collect the eggs.

Now this sounds easier than it is. To you an egg is breakfast. To a chicken it's her child. Chickens do not take kindly to strangers stealing their children. So, into the hen house I go, basket in hand. The chickens start that peculiar 'brrrrraaccckkk' noise that they use when I come in. This always signified war to me. They knew why I was here and they didn't intend to give up without a fight.

Casually I would start down one row of nests. Chickens have a way of turning their heads so they can look at you with one staring, glassy eye. Somehow I find this unnerving (and they know it). Reaching the first nesting hen I reach to stick my hand into her nest like I've seen my grandmother do. 'Brrrrraaccckkk' says the chicken and viciously pecks my hand.

O.K. I'll just move onto the next hen. I thrust my hand into her nest and she flies up, flapping her wings and screeching. Never mind. I'll try the next hen. Up and down both rows I go. All these hens have my number and I emerge from the hen house with just one, precious egg.

Proudly I return to the house to show my grandmother what I've retrieved. "That's O.K. honey," she says. "You've picked up the decoy egg again. Why don't you take a book and ride Starr over to the lake? I'll collect the eggs later."

Well, horseback riding and reading were two of my favorite things so I don't argue, I just go. But tomorrow I know the egg collection has to be done. I vow to myself that next time they won't scare me off.

Every visit to the hen house was the same. The chickens ruled and I ran scared. What was the matter with me? I went across the road and brought the cows home every evening and helped milk them. I helped feed the pigs. I mucked out stalls. What was it about these chickens that intimidated me so?

Many years later I was looking at some old pictures that my mother had. There I was, a toddler, still in diapers and barefoot. There were chickens all around me and I was crying. I pounced on this picture and asked my mother what on earth was I crying about? She showed me another picture taken at the same time. She was off to the side, throwing chicken feed down on the ground around me so the chickens would crowd around me and peck at the feed on the ground by my feet. They thought it was hilarious that I was scared.

At last the mystery was solved. Unknowingly, my parents had traumatized me forever with chickens. To this day I am still afraid of them and take great joy in frying them up or stuffing their little bottoms with dressing and roasting them. Take that chicken, I rule!!

I've always thought that Irish Setters were really beautiful dogs with a good sense of humor. This impression came from an Irish Setter in the obedience class that Princess and I attended when she was nine months old.

One of the advanced commands that we had to master was a 'down-stay'. You put your dog in a down position, told it to stay, turned your back and walked 25 feet before turning around. The dog was supposed to stay until you got to your spot and called it to come to you.

The Irish Setter, 'Maggie', would lay down on command. Her owner would say "Maggie, stay," turn and start walking away. Maggie would crawl toward her retreating back. She would stop, turn and repeat "Maggie, stay!" Well, by the time she got 25 feet away, Maggie was right behind her, still in the down-stay position and I would be on the ground, laughing.

Our instructor would scold me telling me not to laugh at Maggie, it just encouraged her. I could not help it, she was hysterical. Another command Maggie had a problem with was 'down'. Her owner would say "Maggie, down!" She would lay down and then roll over in slow motion onto her back with all four feet sticking up in the air. It was too funny. Sit was another way Maggie showed her individuality. She would start in a sitting position and then sort of roll over on her side and then on her back. Let's face it. Maggie just wasn't taking this seriously.

Maggie frequently got loose, and since this school was in Florida and held outside, we worried she might run in the street and get hit by a car. Not to worry. Maggie wouldn't go far away from her audience. We'd all be trying to catch her, calling her name and trying to grab her. The only way we could get her back was to ignore her. If she thought the game was over she would come back and calmly sit at her owner's side.

49

The Stray Cat & Rabies Shots

In the next cottage to ours in Florida lived an Air Force couple from Texas, John and Delores, who became good friends. One day Delores picked up a stray that changed all our lives. It was a pretty cat with a nice disposition. It appeared at her house one day and just kind of hung around after being fed.

She was outside with her baby son, Cary, and the cat appeared to go nuts. It scratched Cary, and bit her when she tried to pick it up and get it away from Cary. Dolores was afraid that it might have rabies and decided to take it to the base vet to be checked out.

Nobody else was home so she packed Cary, the cat and herself into the car and headed off for the base. When she was getting out of the car at the vet's office, the cat got away from her. She returned home and when I got home told me the story. We decided to go out to the base with our husbands and try to find the cat so that she and Cary wouldn't have to take the painful series of rabies shots.

We drove out there and went in four different directions looking for the cat. I called him and suddenly he appeared. I picked him up and started walking back to the car. Dolores called to the husbands and said I had caught the cat. They ran back to the car, crashing twigs and leaves in their path and all the noise frightened the cat. He leaped from my arms, scratching me on the hand in the process and disappeared into the woods.

Since we didn't have the cat and he had broken the skin on all three of us, Dolores, Cary and me, we all had to get the shots.

Fortunately today, they have a different treatment, but at this time the rabies vaccine was duck embryo and had to be injected into the stomach lining. There was a series of 21 shots to insure coverage. They started on the right lower quadrant of the abdomen and proceeded daily in a clockwise direction.

This was the most painful shot I had ever encountered. Duck embryo is very thick and the shots took a long time to administer. Poor, little Cary, he was only 10 months old! The only good thing about being so young was that he didn't remember that he had to go again tomorrow for another shot. We did.

I had eight shots and then developed an allergy to the vaccine and had to quit. Dolores and Cary had a few more that I did but didn't have to take the entire 21 shots, thank heaven! What a terrible experience.

No, we never saw the cat again.

Frank Adjusts To His New "Family"

After Frank and I bought the house in Willoughby we moved everything and 'everybody' into our new quarters.

Beauregard and Princess had to adjust to a new place, but Frank had the added chore of having to adjust to a whole new "family." Since he had never had pets before, he was sometimes a source of entertainment to me as he dealt with some of the animal things.

He was amazed, and somewhat dismayed, that the dogs wanted to drink out of the toilet. I explained to him that it was a 'dog thing'. Actually, if you think of it, to a dog the toilet is a pretty neat source of water. It's kept reasonable fresh by frequent flushing, (fresher than their water bowl which at best only gets changed twice a day) and it's always ice cold.

The best visual of drinking out of the toilet was when Beauregard would decide to get a drink. To see the cat balanced with his rear paws on the seat, with two front paws inside the toilet bowl on the porcelain, leaning down into the toilet to get a drink. Frank would really flip when he saw this going on. I always expected Beauregard to slip and fall in like the bathtub, but he never did.

One of my friends in Florida had a myna bird. She claimed that he was the smartest thing she had ever seen, including any dog she had ever had.

I pretty much put that claim down to owners' pride. I too believed all my animals were unique, wonderful and extremely smart. She used to tell stories about Charlie, though, that were pretty intriguing. It would be fun to see him, I thought.

She told us about how he would go to the window and watch when it was about time for her to come home. When someone rang the doorbell he would say "someone's at the door" and if it got to be later than 10:00 he would go in his cage, get in his paper bag and go to sleep. She said he was a lot of fun and good company.

One afternoon she invited me and others from work over for lunch. Oh good - I get to meet the bird.

He was in his cage when we got there with the door open. Aline asked him to come out and he did. She told him we were friends from work and introduced all of us. He watched everyone and seemed to take everything in. We were sitting in the living room after lunch and the bird was walking up and down on the back of the couch looking at the TV. Aline had told us stories of how he was very interested in things that happened on TV so I was watching him.

Some people on TV were gathered in a room talking and then they all started leaving, saying "goodbye, see ya later" and things like that. He watched that for a while and then said "where ya all going?" Well I was convinced that he was indeed the smartest bird I'd ever seen!

Excuse Me, Was That A Mouse?

Shortly after we all moved to our new house in Willoughby, Frank and I were on the screened-in porch on the back of the house clearing out some things left by the previous owners in preparation of cleaning the carpet.

Beauregard was out there too, laying down in a patch of sun (of course) with his paws stretched straight out.

Frank picked up a cardboard box and a mouse ran out, went right across both of Beauregard's paws and disappeared out the screen door. Beauregard never moved. He watched the mouse run across his paws and then just watched it go out the door. So much for the idea that cats are natural hunters and will pounce on anything that moves.  Maybe some cats, but the only reaction we got from Beauregard was washing off his paws after the thing was gone. I guess he must have felt soiled.

The Tarantula

This is definitely not a "pet" story, per se, but one that still gives me a chuckle when I think of it.

We had just moved to Florida and found the cottage owned by the retired school teachers. It was close to the base so my Air Force husband could hitchhike to the base easily.

Mr. and Mrs. Armagast, the retired school teachers, had several cottages, all rented to Air Force personnel. Two single cottages and a double with two apartments downstairs and one up.

We lived in one of the single cottages right next door to the Armagast's, and had lived there about a week before I saw "it."

My husband was at the base and I was unpacking more boxes and putting things away. I went into the bedroom with a stack of clothes to put in the dresser when something on the wall up near the ceiling caught my eye. It was the biggest spider I have ever seen. It had to be four inches across with legs as thick as my fingers, no exaggeration. I was scared to go near it and more scared not to. If I didn't kill this thing and it crawled away, I wouldn't know where it was. That was worse than knowing.

I got a chair from the kitchen and a rolled up newspaper and went after it. The darn thing saw me coming and started crawling away. I hit it as hard as I could and it fell to the floor. I hit it several more times (just to make sure) and then I picked it up with the paper and put it aside to show my husband when he got home. I now had the "heebie jeebies" from this thing and made myself some coffee to calm down.

When my husband got home, I showed the thing to him and he was amazed. He took it over to show the Armagast's what I had killed and oh boy were they mad.

It seems that they purchased these things especially to put in the cottages to keep down the bug population. They paid quite a lot for them and weren't happy that I had killed it. My husband told them that they should have told us about their "pet" when we moved in. They agreed and said that they tried not to tell people because most people were a little reluctant to share their home with a tarantula. They always hoped that the thing would not show itself, and because the turnover of tenants was high due to the nature of service life, they mostly got away with it.

I told them that I would put up with the other bugs, thank you very much!! Mosquitos, no-see-ums, and even palmetto bugs were merely a nuisance compared with that awful thing.

Flying Squirrels

Tarantulas were not the only odd thing that these retired school teachers dealt with in Florida.

I was at their house one day having an art lesson (she was a retired art teacher) and something 'flew' out onto the screen porch where we were painting. At first I thought it was a bird, but then it 'flew' closer to me and I saw it was a squirrel! They are native to Florida and have webbed areas between their front and back legs that allows them to glide from place to place. They don't actually fly as in flapping their wings, but they do go from tree to tree in this manner. Although they have a face like a squirrel, they really are kind of scary looking and remind me of a bat.

Mr. and Mrs. Armagast had a pair of them in the house as pets and they appeared quite tame. I was always a little leery of them and never really got close to them. The Armagast's dog, a cute little poodle, was also leery of them and would run under the couch when they started "flying" around.

Look it up in your encyclopedia. I wouldn't kid ya, honest.

Frank Learns About Catnip

Beauregard loved catnip and would overdose if I didn't keep it away from him. An occasional pinch of it was enough to keep him crazy for hours.

Shortly after we were married, I had gone to my volunteer job at the hospital emergency room while Frank and our bass player, Fred, were working on some songs.

Not long after I got to the ER I got a frantic call from Frank saying "something's wrong with Beauregard." I asked what he was doing and Frank said he was running up and down the stairs, twirling in a circle, jumping straight up in the air and looking very wild eyed.

I asked Frank to check on top of the refrigerator and see if the bag of catnip was still there. It was gone so I figured that Beauregard must have seen me put the catnip up there and waited for an opportunity to get it. Getting on top of the refrigerator was a snap for him, only three feet up on the counter and then the other four feet to the top of the fridge.

Beauregard stayed a little nutso for a couple of days and I started storing his catnip inside the refrigerator. That seemed to solve the problem, but I don't think Frank ever got over it.

Not long after the catnip incident, Frank and I were laying on the double recliner watching TV with Beauregard laying on my lap. All of the sudden Beau jumped straight up in the air, turned 90 degrees in mid air and shot across the room. Then just as suddenly, he stopped, and began nonchalantly licking his paws. Frank was very shaken by this and wanted to know "what's wrong with that cat now, has he gotten into the catnip again?" I said, no, that was just cat stuff, they all do that. By the look on Frank's face I could see that he was less than thrilled with this animal he had been forced into living with. Fortunately, as time went on, Frank and Beauregard became great friends and loved to play games with each other and play tricks on each other.

Some of the most fun of having the pets that I did, was watching Frank's reaction to their antics. Having been a pet owner for so long I was used to all this, but he was like a babe in the woods. I think they knew this and took advantage of it.

The Alligator At Dad's Place

Frank's dad spent winters in Palmetto Florida right near Bradenton. The trailer park where he lived has a small lake in the center of it with ducks who almost always had little ones around.

Frank and I were down visiting and had gone for an afternoon bike ride around the lake. We always enjoyed taking bread over to the lake and feeding the ducks, but there didn't seem to be very many there this time.

Snoozing on the bank was a six-foot alligator. Now I knew what had happened to all the ducks. We stopped just short of the alligator as he opened one eye to watch us.

Frank decided to chase it away. I warned him that they were very fast and could probably run faster than he could pedal his bike. He picked up a piece of wood with Spanish moss on it and threw it at the gator while standing not five feet from it.

That gator shot up, turned and hit the water in one motion that took about two seconds. Frank turned very pale as he realized that if the gator had come after him rather than retreating to the water, it would have been on him in less than two seconds. Frank tended to respect my opinions and information about Florida critters after that.

Frank Deals With Some Other Florida Critters

On one visit to Panama City Beach, Frank had his own camera! This was unheard of, I was the camera fiend. Someone had gotten him one for his birthday and he was determined to take some classic shots.

We were staying in a motel at the west end of the beach and had gone for a walk along the surf; Frank took his camera.

Suddenly there were three huge sting rays swimming very close to shore in formation. They were quite scary and I warned Frank to stay out of the water. He was determined to get a good picture of them and began running back and forth on the beach following them to try and get a good snapshot.

After about 10 minutes of this, the sting rays swam away. As we approached our motel someone on the second floor balcony called down to us, "what on earth were you chasing, mister?" We realized then how funny it must have looked, Frank running back and forth like a demented tourist, trying to get the 'perfect picture'.

Beauregard & Pills

When it comes to outsmarting animals, I usually do pretty well. They never like taking their medicine, or taking baths, or having any treatment done to them for any reason. Somehow I always find a way to get them to cooperate. That is until Beauregard developed a heart problem and had to take 1/4 of a 10-milligram heart pill every day.

"Simple," said my vet. "Just break the pill in quarters and put one piece into his mouth, as far back in his throat as you can get it, and keep his mouth closed - he'll eventually swallow it." Oh Yeah? Oh yeah? Wrong!!!

I gently picked Beauregard up and held him in my lap. I gently opened his mouth and tossed in the pill - and lo and behold, it went pretty far back in his throat. I gently closed his little mouth and began to stroke under his chin, something that he dearly loved.

Fifteen minutes went by. I'm stroking under his chin and Boo Boo has swallowed several times and now has his eyes closed and is purring. I give it ten more minutes. He is almost catatonic with drowsiness and contentment, so I put him down on the floor.

He walks slowly away from me, turns his head to the side and goes "ptew." The pill lands at my feet, still in one piece. Where the heck did he put that thing for a half an hour?? This struggle lasted for an entire week until - DUH!, I got the idea to crush the little pill into powder and mix it with his food.

This approach worked wonderfully unless he saw you put the powder in his food. In that case he wouldn't touch it and you would have to make a big show of throwing away the food and giving him fresh. I never could understand why some people call them "dumb animals?"

Sabra - Air Patrol!

Sabra was extremely intelligent and wasn't frightened by anything. She took the clanging and banging of the garbage men with barely an opened eye. Tradesmen, mailmen, salesmen, all were welcomed. Loud cars and motorcycles drew only a glance. She rarely barked unless she perceived a real threat. With one exception.

 Airplanes and Helicopters. They were absolutely not allowed in our yard. She would bark furiously at them and chase them until she reached the end of our property.

If she was in the house they still didn't escape her wrath. She would bark until she could no longer hear them. It was always interesting to me why although she rarely barked at anything else, she picked aircraft as her nemeses.

One of my fondest and last memories of Sabra was the summer night in 1993 when they predicted that "thousands of shooting stars" could be seen that night. I took a blanket outside and laid down in the grass to watch for the shooting stars. After a little while Frank let Sabra out and she made a beeline for me on the blanket. She laid down as close to me as she could get and snuggled up. As it got chilly, I covered us up and we spent a couple of hours watching the shooting stars, all snuggled and covered up with the blanket. In less than two months she was gone from me forever. A victim of sudden unexplained death.

Beauregard hated going to the vet's. Probably because they could get pills to go down and liquid swallowed.

He especially hated it if he had to stay overnight. He was so used to having the run of the house that being caged in a strange place infuriated him.

One time that I recall very well after he had spent the night at the vet's for something, we went to pick him up. We took our Buick that had the velour seats, because I always held Boo Boo so hair wasn't a problem.

When they brought him out, I thought he looked unusually fluffy but thought nothing of it. We got in the car and started home. We only live a quarter of a mile from our veterinary office so Boo Boo had to be quick.

While I was holding him, I suddenly felt very warm in my lap area. I believe he must not have urinated all night at the vet's office, just saved it for me. He drenched me, the velour seat, the floor, everything. Frank was so mad!

While I took a bath and changed clothes, Frank was out in the car trying to clean up the mess. Needless to say, we never picked Beauregard up again at the vet's without a bucket. He was indignant, but I would make him stay in the bucket until we got home.

They were always happy at the vet's office to see him go home, too. According to everyone there he never shut up, just continued to yowl until I came for him.

"Don't Yell At Him, He'll Hide"

Frank took a long time to learn how <u>not</u> to get Beauregard to come to him. (We always think we are training the animals but in our hearts we know - they are training us). When we left the house we would put the animals in "their" room, a room that used to be an attached garage but was converted to an office before we moved there.

Beauregard didn't like going into that room and it took all the skill and guile that you could muster to get him in there. I rarely had a problem, although sometimes he would hide and delay our departure until we could lure him with offers of food. Frank began with the 'firm' approach. "Beauregard, get in the room," he would say. Beauregard would give that "are you talking to me?" look and then turn around and go the other way. If you continued to yell at him (as Frank did) then you would never, and I repeat never, find him.

Beauregard lived in that house for a little more than 10 years and he somehow found a hiding place that we never located. Now, mind you, this was not a huge house. We have a modest, three bedroom, split level. We could search for him room by room, looking everywhere; under, on top of, between - to no avail. Unless he was running from room to room just ahead of our search, he totally outsmarted us. To this day I do not know where he hid when he didn't want to be found.

If Frank was somehow able to yell Beauregard into the room against his will, there was always a payback. We kept our band equipment in their room also and Beauregard instinctively knew which pieces belonged to Frank. When he was mad at Frank he would get on top of one of Frank's amplifier's and either throw up all down the side or find a way to "mark his territory" all over the amp. This would generate more yelling from Frank and more retribution from Beauregard. These two kept up a running battle for 10 years and if I had to pick a winner I would have to say that Beauregard usually came out on top. I think they both secretly enjoyed the challenge.

65

Cocoa - Guard Dog In Reverse?

My good friends Chuck and Joanie have a three year old, mostly Husky type, dog named Cocoa. She has a very unique personality. They purchased her at the Humane Society as a young puppy so it's hard to say what kind of early environment she had.

Cocoa does not like men very well, especially Joanie's brother Tom (sorry Tom) and come to think of it, isn't especially fond of women either. When you come into their house, they have to keep her in another room. After you are there for a while and seated in the family room, they can let her loose. She comes up to you and if you reach for her slowly she will allow you to pet her. Everything seems fine, but don't get out of your chair!!

If you attempt to go to the bathroom or heaven forbid, try to leave and go home - she attacks. She barks and growls and it appears that she would really physically attack if they didn't intervene. Chuck and Joanie are at a loss for explaining her conduct. To their knowledge she was never mistreated or traumatized by anyone and they have tried to change her demeanor. I told Joanie, Cocoa is just a little confused. She thinks she is supposed to prevent people from leaving the house, unlike a trained guard dog who would try to prevent people from entering.

December 1998 - a breakthrough! Cocoa allowed a houseful of people to come to celebrate Chuck's birthday. We were all allowed to move freely about the house and were even allowed to leave. Yes, Tom was there too!

66

"We'll Have One of These and One of Those"

After Sabra died, I thought I wouldn't survive. The pain was unbearable but I wasn't ready to get another dog.

Somewhere around mid-October we started talking about getting a puppy. The hurt hadn't gone away, but the longing for the collie companionship grew stronger.

We located the breeder that we were interested in and they did have puppies ready to go around Christmas. We drove out to see them and fell in love.

This was a big litter of 10. We gushed over the puppies and then the breeders showed us the parents. The father was a three-year-old sable and the mother was a young tri-color. The mother, Velvet, came into the living room and made a beeline for Frank. He was sitting on the floor and she laid down next to him and put her head in his hand. I had already paid for a sable when Frank said, "I think we want one of these too," meaning a tri-color. I wrote another check and they said we could pick the puppies up on Christmas Eve.

As we were driving back to town, we were remarking about how we must have lost our minds buying two puppies. What a job. Cleaning up, training and grooming one dog was a chore, how would we handle two? We've never regretted the decision. They are wonderful, intelligent dogs who are very close and are great company for each other.

They have very different personalities. Tangie, the sable, is very 'don't touch me unless I want to be touched', while Lexie is a big teddy bear who loves to cuddle and curl up with you. Tangie now weighs 75 pounds and Lexie 60. They both want to sleep with us and even though we have a queen size bed it sure gets crowded with all four of us in there!

67

Beauregard & The Doll House

Once when Beauregard was "missing" I walked past my doll house which is quite big. Out of the corner of my eye I saw something that didn't look just right. I stopped to check it out and there was Beauregard, lying in the doll house living room with all the furniture still in place. This was really a sight because he was a very big cat and how he could enter the house and then lay down without disturbing anything was pretty interesting.

I went for my camera and was able to get a couple of shots before he indignantly left. He was among the missing for the rest of the day so he was probably mad that I had made fun of him by taking the pictures and calling Frank to come and look.

Beauregard was very sensitive and didn't like to be made fun of. We learned the hard way not to make him mad enough to retaliate - at least we learned in time to save the amplifier from total destruction.

My father was known as a "softie" when it came to animals. He once ran over someone's tree lawn to avoid hitting a bird. I guess that's where I get it. When I was little, I was always bringing home hurt animals for my Daddy to fix. I remember one time I found a bird that's wings were frozen so it couldn't fly. I brought it home but my mother said we couldn't keep it in the house. She knew that once its little wings thawed out it would start flying. We put it in the garage in a box with some rags in a warm corner. Since my Dad was working late my mother forgot to tell him about the bird. Next morning when my Dad opened the garage door to leave for work, the bird, who by now was totally unfrozen, flew out in his face and scared him. In a moment, though, he recovered. He had figured out that it was just another one of Bev's hurt animals.

That's my only explanation for Homer the Seagull. We were living in our first little cottage in Panama City at the time, and I had taken a walk on our small beach. I saw a dog that had something in its mouth. When it saw me come closer it dropped what it had and ran away. On closer inspection I found it was a seagull. He was not dead but his wing was broken. Poor thing, I thought. I picked it up and brought it back to the house. I put it in a box and placed it in the open laundry room. When my husband came home, I showed him the seagull and told him his name was 'Homer'. He told me that the thing would probably die because we wouldn't be able to feed it and with a broken wing it was helpless. I refused to give up on Homer and tried to nurse him back to health.

After a week or so he was walking around and looking very good. I thought if I could just get his wing mended then he could fly again.

One morning I looked for him and he was gone from the laundry room. I walked out on the beach and there he was sitting on the beach. I walked up to him and picked him up. Now he had a broken leg, apparently he had been attacked again by the dog. I brought him back to the laundry room. Now I was faced with a terrible dilemma. How could I justify trying to keep this poor thing alive?

When my husband came home, I asked him to check Homer and do whatever had to be done. Homer disappeared. I didn't ask what he did with him. I didn't want to know. Sometimes the creatures just can't be saved. I wonder if my Dad would believe that.

Our next door neighbor, Marian, had two Yorkshire Terriers, Petey and Rufus. They were her constant companions and we would see them outside running around often. Soon after we moved there Rufus died.

Petey was Sabra's buddy. She wanted so much to play with him, but he was a little afraid of her size. She would lay down in the driveway and make herself as small as she could so as to not scare Petey and he allowed her to stay near him under those circumstances. Sometimes he would bark at her until she walked over toward him and then he would back off, again intimidated by her size. It was cute when they took a walk together into the back yard. Little six pound, six inch tall Petey and 78 pound, two foot tall Sabra taking a stroll. Petey had to hop and run to keep up with Sabra walking.

Sabra loved our neighbor Marian. Whenever Sab would go outside, she would end up at Marian's side door looking in for her. I would watch her as she stood there patiently waiting. When Sabra's tail would start wagging I knew Marian had seen her and was heading to the door to give her a treat.

Marian was Sabra's "babysitter" on the occasions when we had to go away and couldn't take her. She said Sabra was so easy to take care of. Marian would go over several times a day and let her out and feed her. She said Sab would never leave the yard and was completely obedient to everything Marian said. Like I said, she was the smartest dog I've ever seen.

When we lost Sabra, Marian was devastated. She had lost her buddy. Shortly afterwards she made a donation to the Humane Society dedicated to the memory of Petey, Rufus, Princess, Randi, Sabra and Beauregard. Between us we had lost so many beloved pets.

Beauregard Stomps

You could always tell when Beauregard was mad at someone or something. You know how cats are perceived to be light on their feet and stealthy? Well, Beauregard could make more noise walking down the kitchen steps if he were annoyed about something.

You would hear this 'stomp, stomp, stomp' and one of us would say, "oh oh, Beauregard is mad again." Frank would run and check his amplifiers to see if Boo Boo was mad at him.

The dogs took it all in stride. They always pretended to be ruled by him but they really only tolerated his bullying. I have one picture where Sabra as a young puppy has Boo Boo down with one paw across his neck. The look on his face is pure astonishment.

Tangie & Lexie - The Girls On The Beach

When Tangie and Lexie were one year old, we borrowed our friend Bob's van and drove to Florida. We rented a beach house on the Gulf of Mexico and settled in for two weeks of sun, sand and no phones.

Our girls were not completely house trained, rarely went in the car and had never been away from home so we didn't know what to expect. They were angels! They immediately took to riding in the van and stretched out and slept most of the time. We made stops about every two hours and they would drink some water, eat a couple bites of food and do their thing and be ready to ride again.

When we got to the beach house, they were amazing. The house was on stilts and had a deck completely around it. It was total paradise. The girls were so good, they never in the entire two weeks had an accident in the house, they thoroughly enjoyed the deck and loved the beach. They were like seasoned little travelers and were a joy to be with. I have some incredibly funny video of an encounter they had with a ghost crab. The thing was about two inches across, but managed to hold off both dogs until it could get to its hole. I would not hesitate to take them again on any vacation, they were great.

After the first day the temperature rose to the 80's and 90's. We weren't worried about the dogs because they could come in the house or stay out on the deck, whatever they wanted to do.

After a 90-degree morning we missed Lexie. We found her in one of the bedrooms standing in the corner facing the wall. I called her and she just stayed there. We went to her and found her to be very hot to the touch. I cooled her off with towels and she began acting O.K. From then on we had to watch her carefully. She would lay out on the deck no matter what the temperature. We had to call her and make her come in periodically so she would not have another episode. What a character!

Beach Babies

We took another Florida trip to the beach when Tangie & Lexie were two. This time we went to Carrabelle and rented a condo.

Although we had to load them in the van and drive to the beach (about 10 minutes) it was still an enjoyable vacation. They loved the beach and we spent hours walking and picnicking there. Tangie & Lexie became favorites amongst the other condo residents in our walks around the complex and we figured that we had pets that we could take anywhere who would enjoy the same things we enjoyed; ocean, sand and sun. Oh, were we wrong!!

 When Tangie & Lexie were three we again rented a house on the Panhandle Gulf Coast, this time on St. George Island, truly a paradise.

Unfortunately, a tropical storm decided to destroy our vacation. The first five days there it rained and the wind blew like fury. We would take the girls to the beach and the sand would blow in their eyes and the gusty wind would try to knock them over - they hated it and so did we.

When we had three more days of vacation, the island was evacuated. The tropical storm had increased its fury and threatened to turn into a full-blown hurricane. We had to leave and start back early for home. It was a terrible vacation weather wise but we still enjoyed getting away from the pressures of work. This bad experience with the weather in Florida would come back to haunt us.

Our Motorhome Denizens

We had been borrowing our friend Bob's van for three summers and it worked well for traveling with the "girls," but we really needed something bigger as they continued to grow.

We bought a motorhome and set out for our first vacation to - where else - St. George Island. We always vacation in October in Florida because the weather is much more receptive for our dogs and still more than acceptable for us. In fact my favorite months to visit Florida are April and October, less humidity and more tolerable temperatures, 70's and 80's.

We had already rented a beach house but used the motorhome to travel in. It was heaven. All the great things that the van had and more!! A bed for us and one for the dogs!! A shower!! A bathroom!! A kitchen!! Oh boy, I was going to enjoy vacationing in this.

We got to Florida (it was October) and the weather was unseasonably warm. Daytime temps in the high 90's. The girls were miserable. All they wanted to do was stay in the house in the air conditioning. Their last beach experience was not forgotten either. They had no interest in walking on the beach even in the evening after it cooled off. They remembered that sand blew in their eyes and stung their bodies. No way were they going on the beach.

Now we have a real dilemma. Our beach baby, great travelers, wonderful companions were acting like someone else's dogs. Who were these creatures and what had they done with our darlings??

Our next vacation would be a real test. Would we able to travel to Florida again? Would they make our life miserable?

Another Try At A Beach Vacation

We decide to try again at a Florida beach vacation. How many times can you be forced out of Florida by bad weather? We work hard to get this time off and by golly we're gonna' get our vacation in the sun.

We drive to Panama City Florida to attend a surprise 75th birthday party for my good friend Barb. We park the motorhome in a beautiful campground right on St. Andrews Bay. The girls love it and the weather is ideal. After the party we are going down to Carrabelle to stay in a campground right on the Gulf.

The night before we are to leave for Carrabelle it begins to rain. And rain. And rain. And blow. Then we find out that a hurricane is moving toward the gulf coast.

We pack up the next morning in the sunshine and head for Carrabelle. We are all set up there, right on the Gulf of Mexico and the weather is wonderful. The girls are walking across the street to the beach without complaint and we are happy knowing that they have forgotten the bad memories of the beach and we are back on track.

We have a screen room which we attach to the motorhome to give us extra room (two adults and two collies in a motorhome is a riot). We are sitting in the screen room watching TV when a weather bulletin comes on warning residents of the Gulf Coast Panhandle region of the impending hurricane.

Since it is now pouring rain, along with thunder, lightning and winds strong enough to take down our screen room, we decide it would be prudent to pack up and leave the area. The girls are barking and whining with every crash of thunder and we are certain that they will not take kindly to another trip to the beach! Are we star crossed or what? All we want to do is take a little relaxing trip to the beach in our motorhome.

Sabra & The Fireplace

Sabra was always enchanted with fire. If Frank would go over to the fireplace and open the fireplace screen she would immediately go over and sit beside him. He would have to push her away in order to build the fire. She was that close.

Once the fire was laid, she would either lay in front of it, or sit and stare into the flames. Sometimes I had to make her come away from it because she was so hot, her fur was hot to the touch.

At times she would lay in front of the fire with her head on the hearth stone. It was spooky. We never figured out the attraction of the fire for her. None of our other dogs had ever shown the same fascination.

Christmas Cat

Beauregard, as you've come to know, was not an ordinary cat. He didn't do cute cat things, he didn't answer when called, he didn't obey any order, he spoke to you only if he so desired and he did mischievous and sometimes spiteful things. He was however, lovable, amusing, and totally unforgettable.

One Christmas I wanted to take pictures of him with some sort of Christmas theme. I tried a Santa hat but he would have none of that. So I took a long piece of thick red yarn (the kind you use at Christmas to tie around packages) and made a bow around his neck. Before I could even get the camera, he had the yarn in his mouth trying to get it off.

I took the pictures anyway because the expression on his face is priceless. His disgust is evident. We called him "Christmas Cat."

We Bring Our Christmas Puppies Home

Tangie and Lexie were ready to go to their new home on Christmas Eve. We were so excited because we had gifted each other with these marvelous presents and wanted to see them.

We drove out to the breeder's in a terrible snowstorm to pick up our "babies." After all the paperwork transfer and instructions we were ready to head for home.

I got in the back seat with pillows and blankets to keep the babies warm and to contain them. We had about a half an hour ride home with regular weather, more like 45 minutes this night. They drove me crazy.

The tri-color, Lexie, cried and wined and wiggled and tried to get off the blankets, while Tangie kept opening her mouth really wide and making an "ack" noise as she tried to get car sick all over me. I was ready to switch places with Frank and let him hold the little darlings.

We took our little Christmas presents over to our friends Carolyn and Charlie where they promptly fell asleep in their new portable pen. The "playpen" we called it. In a couple of hours after they woke from their nap, we all cuddled them, oohed and aahed over them and generally began the spoiling process. At midnight we took them to their new home and wished us all a "Merry Christmas."

79

Beauregard & Food

When Boo Boo was about 10, his kidneys began to fail, not unusual at his age. Our vet recommended that we start him on kidney disease food which is low in ash and has other important advantages for animals with his problem. She also gave me a recipe for making home made food for him. This was all well and good and Beauregard seemed to like the food all right, but he was eating less now, probably due to the bland taste of it.

He never lost his taste for chicken, and since we eat almost no red meat at our house, pretty much the standard fare at the Hess's is turkey, fish or chicken. We also like to watch TV while we eat, so our meals are taken in front of the TV on trays.

Beauregard would get on the arm of my chair and with every bite I took he would hook my arm with his paw and try to pull it to his mouth. The only way I could survive at dinner time was to make sure that I kept a piece of chicken or turkey already cut into little tiny pieces so I could keep feeding him as I went along. He never tried this with Frank, only me. So you can see who the real sucker is.

"Bring In A Urine Sample"

Sabra, my smartest collie and probably the most dignified, was a very private individual when it came to the 'calls of nature'. She did not like to be watched and would go the farthest corner of the property to do her business.

Once when she was sick, the vet told us to bring in a urine sample so they could run some tests to determine what was going on. I asked, (innocently enough knowing how she was) "how can I do that, she doesn't like to be watched." They told me to just follow her with a pie plate and when she squatted, stick it under her. Seems simple enough, right?

Sabra and I go outside for a walk, me armed with an aluminum pie plate. Every time she tried to squat I would try to stick this pie plate under her and of course it would make a rattling noise. She would jump up and look back at me with an expression of disbelief. What on earth was I trying to do? We spent 20 minutes outside and six attempts at a pie plate catch to no avail.

Next day we go outside, this time I'm armed with a plastic Frisbee. I stalk her and as she squats I time my Frisbee thrust for a tiny moment after she begins. She jumps up again in disbelief, but as I look in my Frisbee I see several drops of precious urine. I have succeeded!

I take the precious few drops of urine to the vet's office and they say, "this is it?" "Don't knock it," I say. "You're lucky to get this much."

For weeks after Sabra would not squat until she was far enough away from me to be sure I wouldn't stick anything under her, and always looked back to see what I was doing after she squatted. Hum, they still call them 'dumb animals'.

81

Beauregard & The Doves

When Frank and I got married and bought our new home, we all moved in, Frank and I along with Princess and Beauregard. That was enough shock for one previously 'petless' person like Frank, but after the loss of Princess and adopting Randi and then adding Sabra, Frank's children were moving to California and wanted us to take their pair of doves. I was not keen on the idea but really didn't want to say anything since Frank had so readily agreed to my pets.

We took the doves and named them Mach (for macho man) and Sarah. We had them for a couple of years and then they started having kids. First one egg hatched and we had a baby that rapidly grew into an adult that the male no longer wanted in the cage. We purchased another cage and, lo and behold, Sarah produced another fertile egg. This one grew just as rapidly and Mach soon threw it out also.

Now we had two pair of doves. One pair in a hanging cage that Beauregard didn't pay any attention to, and the other pair in a cage sitting on a TV tray.

One day I observed Beauregard nonchalantly going over to the TV tray to see what all the commotion was about. He stood on his hind legs but still couldn't see into the cage. Well he decided to take his best shot. He stretched his body as tall as he could and his paw would just barely reach into the cage. He was feeling around in there blindly just hoping to grab hold of something. The doves, who were on the opposite side of the cage watching all this fumbling around, suddenly had enough. They both came over to where Boo Boo's paw was and pecked it at the same time. You never saw a little paw jump back so fast. He was indignant! He must have washed that paw for two hours.

We were going on vacation that summer and we took our menagerie into the vet's for boarding. Two dogs, a cat and four birds. Our vet mentioned that he knew someone that loved and had a houseful of birds that might like our four. We said, "by all means. If you know someone who really wants them, they're gone!" When we came back from vacation, the two pair of doves had been adopted. We visited their new home and they must have been in birdie heaven. They had their own room (with all the other parakeets and canaries) and they were free to fly wherever. We were satisfied that they had a good home.

It is December 1998, the book has been finished for over a year and is waiting for Cousin Dick to complete the illustrations (sorry, Cuz, I had to get in a dig). Frank and I are in the local pet food store buying dog food for the spoiled babies when destiny strikes.

I walk past the area where the rescued stray cats are kept. As I glance in, I stop dead in my tracks. There is Beauregard reincarnated.

"Frank" I say sharply, "come here." He comes back to where I am and takes a look. "Ohmigod" he says, "Beauregard." So it isn't only me. This seven-month-old kitten looks almost identical.

We adopt and bring her home and name her "Cassie." The fun is just beginning. She takes one week to acquaint herself with the layout of the house (while maintaining her own quarters in the spare bedroom) and then just asserts herself and takes over.

Tangie and Lexie and scared to death of her and run away when she comes near. Now the sight of a 78 pound and a 68-pound dog each running from a six-pound kitten is really something.

After the first few days the dogs begin to accept her and actually seem to enjoy watching her antics. It has been many years since the kittenhood of Beauregard and I too am enjoying her antics. She is a good addition to our family. Now the question remains. Will she also travel well in the motorhome?

One of Cassie's "fun" things to do in her new home is to run full speed everywhere. She likes running into the bathroom, into the tub, out of the tub and full speed ahead to the next room.

I know you can, of course, already see what's coming. But so did I and tried very hard to prevent it happening.

I was taking a bath when Cassie came in at regular speed and came over to the tub to see what was going on. I showed her that there was water in the tub and it was not something to jump in to. She seemed to take it in and understand.

A couple of days later Frank was in the bathroom shaving before he got into the tub in which he had already drawn his bath water.

Into the bathroom streaked Cassie full speed toward the tub. She stopped and put her paws on the rim of the tub and looked in. "You don't want to do that!" said Frank in vain as she dove in. He quickly plucked her out and wrapped her in a towel and brought her, purring, to me to be dried. None the worse for the wear she allowed me to dry her and then streaked off to her next adventure.

The question is . . . , will she do it again?

Is That An Air Raid Siren?

Cassie was taken to our regular vet as soon after we had brought her home as an appointment could be obtained. "That sure is a funny looking collie," Doc said as he peered into her carrier. "Come on out of there sweetie," he said.

He checked her over and remarked what a nice cat she was and how loudly she purred and how content she seemed. He even had trouble hearing her heart beat over the loud purring.

The stitches from her spaying had not dissolved as they had told me, so doc said he would take her in back and remove the stitches and give her a booster shot that was due.

A couple of minutes after the technician had taken her off to the back, loudly purring, we heard what appeared to be an air raid siren growing louder and higher in decibel with each passing second. It seemed to go on forever and increased in intensity. "Ohmigosh," I said, "is that Cassie?"

We got our answer when two very astonished looking men entered the exam room. Doc with a sort of sheepish grin and the technician, pale and shaky, carrying a loudly purring Cassie. "Was that . . . " I started to ask. "Yes, that was Cassie," said Doc. "It's a good thing we weren't putting stitches in instead of taking them out. I'd have been arrested for cruelty."

So now I come to the end of my pet stories. My heart is full of the memories of all the wonderful pets I have written about. I am cheered by the fact that I still have the two "spoiled babies," Tangie and Lexie to carry on the tradition. They already have given us joy, laughter, companionship and unconditional love. Perhaps they will be the subjects of another book ... let's see ... "Tangie & Lexie, The Saga Continues" ... hum, I like it.
The End.

Or is it just a New Beginning?

1998 P.S. And now there is Cassie.

This book is lovingly inscribed to anyone who has ever been owned by an animal, for no matter how hard we may try to tell ourselves to the contrary - they do indeed own us and own our hearts forever.